iLead

little black book on leadership

Developed in conjunction with the iLead
Leadership Development Framework Initiative.

ISBN: 1493547402
ISBN-13: 978-1493547401

Dedication

This book is dedicated to every student, every person, and every individual who desires to be the best. You are the only **YOU** in the world! You have the potential to **change** the world one thought, **one** conversation, **one** interaction, **one** person at a time. Always remember the power of **one**. Everyday strive to live your life with discipline, courage, and integrity.

Leadership Development Program • Cultivating the Students of Today to be Influential Leaders of Tomorrow

iLead Creed

I am a leader
I accept responsibility and ownership
Of my actions and my words
I will not make excuses for poor decisions
Every day I will strive to be an example
In what I do and what I say
I will live my life
With discipline, courage, and integrity
I am a leader

TABLE OF CONTENTS

WHAT IS LEADERSHIP?

Simply put **leadership** is <u>**exerting influence**</u> on others.

This *influence* can be **positive** or **negative**.

> Some people use their influence to damage, hurt, and make life more difficult for others.

> Others use their influence to **encourage**, help, and make life **easier** for others.

<u>**Everyone**</u> is a leader because we <u>**all**</u> influence those around us.

Positive *leadership* is realizing your *own* **worth** and **potential** so *clearly* that you are **motivated** to do the same for *others*.

When you **embrace** *leadership* you realize that <u>**you**</u> <u>**can**</u> make a **difference**.

You believe the world will be better because of your influence.

LL1: Discipline

Discipline Defined: training that **corrects** or **molds** an individual's **thinking** or moral **character**.

Discipline is training yourself to do what you **NEED** to do **NOT** what you **WANT** to do.

Discipline teaches you that your **decisions** *can't* be based on **feelings** and **emotions**.

Many times in life you will need to **choose** to do right even though you may not feel like it.

Discipline requires you to establish the right **habits**.

Habits are routines you have followed or choices that you have made so often you almost don't think about them anymore you just do them.

There are **good** habits and **bad** habits.

Good Habits **empower** you and make it easier to do the right thing <u>all</u> the time.

<u>**Two**</u> <u>types of *Discipline*</u>:

Self-Imposed Discipline: this begins with <u>**you**</u> taking the initiative to discipline and teach yourself in order to be successful.

Authority-Imposed Discipline: this begins with <u>**someone else**</u> disciplining you or teaching you in order to help you become successful.

If you don't *discipline* yourself, someone else <u>**WILL**</u> do it for you.

Think About It

What are some areas in which you need to *discipline* yourself in order to become a better leader, student, or person?

LL2: Courage

Courage Defined: a state of mind that allows a person to face *difficulty, danger, pain, etc.*

Courage allows you to **choose** or **act** when you are **afraid** or when **adversity** is present.

Courage is doing what is **right** when you are scared of the **result** or **outcome**.

Many people **know** what is right; but less have the *courage* to **choose** what is right.

FACT: you will be faced with difficult decisions and circumstances in life.
The chances are you will *know* what to do.
The question is, **"will you have the *courage* to do it?"**

Think About It

Give an example of a career in which a person must possess courage. Why is courage so important for them in order to be successful at their job?

Why do you think courage will be so important as you get older?

LL3: Integrity

Integrity Defined: the quality of being upright, the state of being whole.

Integrity means you are **consistent** with your actions, values, decisions, expectations.

Integrity is <u>essential</u> when building structures. The raw materials that are chosen must be free from *defect*, *strong*, *whole* in nature.
If the materials selected to build don't have integrity, the building or structure will fall apart.

The same principle applies in our lives.
When *integrity* is absent the different parts of our lives will begin to fall apart.

The *foundation* of our *character* should be our **integrity**.
Our thoughts and actions should be free from *defect*.
Our desire to do right **ALL** the time should be *strong*.
We must be *wholly* committed to having good values.
Doing this we can prevent our lives from falling apart...all by possessing **integrity**!

When a person acts differently when he or she is with different groups there is a **lack** of *integrity*.

Integrity is doing the **right** thing no matter **where you are** or **who you are with.**

Think About It

What would you think about a person who tells you one thing then does something entirely different?

Are there currently areas in your life where you act the right way when you are with certain people and the wrong way when you are with another group?

LL4: Initiative

Initiative Defined: the power to **act, take charge**, or **volunteer** without being asked or told to.

Don't wait for an invitation in life.

Let your attitude _always_ be "**I WILL**"

It's very easy to sit back and be like everyone else; **STEP UP!**

It's really easy to _think_ about doing something good or nice but few embrace the opportunity to **act**!

Be the **spark** that starts the **fire**. One little spark can create a fire that can become uncontrollable. Take **initiative** in life!

Think About It

Think of a way you can take the *initiative* and make things better at home.

Think of goal that you have for yourself. How could you take the initiative in achieving that goal?

LL5: Gratitude & Service

Gratitude Defined: being **thankful**, to **appreciate**

We have **so many things** to be *thankful* for.

Gratitude all begins with my **attitude**.

When we focus our minds on that which is **positive** we will find it easier to find **many** things to be thankful for.

We must train ourselves to think about what we **have** *not* what we **don't have**.

When I truly appreciate what I have and I am grateful, I will want to focus on **service** and **helping** others.

Service focuses on making life **better** and/or **easier** for others.

Think About It

List at least **6** things you can be thankful for.

Think of some easy ways you could serve others.

LL6: Enthusiasm

Enthusiasm Defined: **excitement** of feeling, something that creates intense **enjoyment** or **interest**.

We all have things that we naturally enjoy. The reality is we don't get to do the things that we enjoy the most all the time. If we only have enthusiasm when we do things we naturally enjoy MUCH of our lives could be dull and boring.

Enthusiasm is a **choice**.

When we **choose** to be enthusiastic we turn **any** situation or circumstance into a **great opportunity** to live and have a richer fuller life.

Enthusiasm is **contagious**.

People are naturally drawn to people who **choose** to be enthusiastic because of the *positive energy* they create.

Think About It

Think of a person you know that chooses to be enthusiastic.

Why do you like to be around him or her?

LL7: Perseverance

Perseverance Defined: to continue doing something despite difficulty or delay in success.

FACT: You **<u>WILL</u>** have problems and sometimes life will **<u>not</u>** be easy.

FACT: It is how you respond during those difficult times that will **<u>define</u>** who you are and **<u>determine</u>** what you will be.

Never, never, never give up!

Perseverance is staying **committed** to your values and what you **know** to be right when **<u>difficult</u>** situations arise.

Perseverance is not giving up when things get hard.

Think About It

Think about a time you did something but it took you multiples attempts to achieve.

How did it feel when you were finally able to complete it?

How would you have felt if you gave up and never tried to complete it again?

LL8: Humility

Humility is:

A true assessment of your **worth**.
A true assessment of the **worth of others**.

A true and **honest reflection** about *yourself*:
the **good** and the **not so good**.

Refusing to act like a **know it all**.

Remaining **teachable** no matter how much
you learn.

Always being willing to **serve others** no
matter what position or title you may hold.

Refusing to think I am better than someone
else

A **king** who cleans the **toilet**.

Think About It

Think of a person who has a very important role but still takes time to serve others.

Is a person who brags all the time or talks about how great they are humble? Why or Why not?

LL9: Purpose

Purpose is:

The motivating factor behind a person's action or behaviour.

The reason you **act** or **do** the things you do.

Every individual needs *purpose* in life. We need a **reason** to live.

Everyone has goals and dreams they wish to achieve, but our purpose in life should go beyond that.

Our purpose should be **greater** than ourselves.

The lives of others should be **easier** and/or **better** because of *our purpose*.

Think About It

What goals or dreams do you have for your life ?

What occupation would you like to pursue?

What is going to be your purpose in life?

How can you join your occupation with your purpose?

LL10: Manners

Manners are:

Good behaviors *anyone* can learn.

Skills you should use the **rest** of your life.

A way to communicate **respect** for yourself and others.

A **guaranteed** way to bring **positive** attention to yourself.

Manners can also be known as **etiquette**.

Some situations may require you to have a different set of manners.
 Always do your best!

Everyday Manners & Etiquette

1. Wait your turn & don't interrupt. If it is an emergency say "Excuse me" before you say anything else.
2. No name calling or talking bad about people. If you can't say something nice, don't say anything at all.
3. Always greet others. We meet people all the time. Smile, shake their hand, introduce yourself, try to make an effort to remember their name.
4. Please, thank you, you're welcome. Use your power words!
5. Clean up after yourself. If you made a mess, clean it up. If you really want to stand out, clean up the mess even though you didn't make it.
6. Display good sportsmanship. No bragging if you win and no whining if you lose. Always shake hands with opponents.
7. Receive a compliment. If someone gives you a compliment receive it and say "thank you very much. That means a lot to me."

8. Give a compliment. Always look for the good in others and tell them when you notice it.
9. Open and hold doors for others.
10. Respect differences. Everyone is unique and different. Don't treat someone unfairly because they are different than you.
11. Always sit up straight and don't slouch in your chair. You show people how much you are listening with your body language.
12. Don't use profanity.
13. Always keep your conversation clean and appropriate.
14. When you enter and exit a building always do so in an orderly quiet fashion.
15. If a lady or adult comes in a room and there is nowhere to sit, offer them your seat.

Think About It

Do you say Yes Maam, No maam, Yes sir, No sir?

Do you wait until others are finished speaking before you speak?

Do you let others go first?

Do you let ladies go first?

Do you compliment and find the good in people?

Do you follow the rules or an establishment?

Do you treat ALL people with respect?

Don't Believe the Lies!

Lie **ONE**: Your worth is determined by how **strong** you are or your **physical** abilities.
Truth: Your **mental strength** is more important than your physical strength.

Lie **TWO**: Your worth is tied to how much **money** you have or the **position** you can obtain.
Truth: Your worth is determined by how much you **enrich the lives of others**.

Lie **THREE**: Your worth is determined by how **popular** you are.
Truth: Your worth is determined by making decisions that may be **unpopular**.

Think About It

Which lie do you find yourself believing the most? Why?

What are some ways you can safeguard your mind from believing these lies?

THE MOST IMPORTANT WORDS

As you finish the little black book the most important words you can remember are:

You are one of a kind.

There is no one else like you in the entire world!
You are the only you!

Be content to be yourself, but never be content to stay the way you are.

Always remember how special you are, but always look for ways to become a better you.

Always be confident in who you are.
Walk with your head up and be proud of who you are.

At the same time, let other people praise you. Don't be self-absorbed and talk about yourself all the time.

People who are truly self-confident don't need to go around talking about themselves all the time.

Learn how to listen to others. Make an effort to find out about other people and show interest in them.

Remember:

You are the only **YOU** in the world! You have the potential to **change** the world one thought, **one** conversation, **one** interaction, **one** person at a time. Always remember the power of **one**. Everyday strive to live your life with **discipline**, **courage**, and **integrity**.

Recommended Usage

The little black book on leadership has been specifically designed to be used in the following ways:

First, *the little black book has been created as a handbook to provide individuals with quick personal lessons, which when implemented in their lives, will allow them to unleash their fullest potential as a leader and a person. These lessons are meant to be revisited as often as possible not read once and put on a shelf to be remembered no more. The short design of the content allows the reader to read the lessons multiple times in an effort to establish the principles as daily habits in their lives.*

Secondly, *the little black book is designed to be implemented in the context of a small group environment with a facilitator who can expand on the topics and offer real life illustrations to add depth to the content.*

For more information or to connect
with the iLead initiative visit:
www.ileadframework.weebly.com
or email:
ilead.framework@gmail.com